Lab Rules

© 2001 Willow Creek Press
Photos © Lee Thomas Kjos

Published by Willow Creek Press, P.O. Box 147, Minocqua, Wisconsin 54548

Compiled and edited by Andrea Donner
Design by Patricia Bickner Linder

For information on other Willow Creek Press titles, call 1-800-850-9453

Library of Congress Cataloging-in-Publication Data
Library of Congress Cataloging-in-Publication Data

Kjos, Lee Thomas.
Lab rules : virtues of the canine character / photographs by Lee
Thomas Kjos.
p. cm.
ISBN 1-57223-299-4 (hardcover : alk. paper)
1. Labrador retriever--Pictorial works. 2. Labrador
retriever--Quotations, maxims, etc. I. Title.
SF429.L3 K57 2001
636.752'7'0222--dc21
2001004854

Printed in Canada

Lab Rules

Virtues of the Canine Character

Photographs by Lee Thomas Kjos

Willow Creek® PRESS

Determination

*Nothing in the world can take the place
of persistence . . . Persistence and
determination are omnipotent.*

—ATTRIBUTED TO CALVIN COOLIDGE

Great works are performed, not by strength, but by perseverance.

—SAMUEL JOHNSON

Every noble work is at first impossible.

—THOMAS CARLYLE

'Tis known by the name of perseverance in a good cause—
and of obstinacy in a bad one.

—LAURENCE STERNE

Joyful

All animals, except man, know that the principal business of life is to enjoy it.

—SAMUEL BUTLER

. . . joy delights in joy.

—William Shakespeare

Contentment is natural wealth.

—SOCRATES

We know nothing of tomorrow; our business is to be good and happy today.

—SYDNEY SMITH

Clownish

Dogs laugh, but they laugh with their tails.

—MAX FORRESTER EASTMAN

The great thing about a dog is that you may make a fool of yourself with him and not only will he not scold you, but he will make a fool of himself too.

—SAMUEL BUTLER

Dogs don't mind being photographed in compromising situations.

—ELLIOTT ERWITT

Patient

*To know how to wait is the
great secret of success.*

—JOSEPH MARIE DE MAISTRE

Patience is the art of hoping.

—Luc de Clapiers Vauvenargues

Desire

Live that thou mayest desire to live again.

—FRIEDRICH WILHELM NIETZSHE

The thirst of desire is never filled, nor fully satisfied.

—MARCUS TULLIUS CICERO

It is not strange that desire should so many years outlive performance.

—WILLIAM SHAKESPEARE

Devoted

Dog: A kind of additional or subsidiary deity designed to catch the overflow and surplus of the world's worship.

—AMBROSE BIERCE

I am because my little dog knows me.

—GERTRUDE STEIN

If you pick up a starving dog and make him prosperous, he will not bite you. This is the principal difference between a dog and man.

—MARK TWAIN

Intelligent

All knowledge, the totality of all questions and all answers, is contained in the dog.

—Franz Kafka

The dog has an enviable mind. It remembers the nice things in life and quickly blots out the nasty.

—BARBARA WOODHOUSE

The charming relations I have had with a long succession of dogs result from their happy spontaneity. Usually they are quick to discover that I cannot see or hear. Truly, as companions, friends, equals in opportunities of self-expression, they unfold to me the dignity of creation.

—HELEN KELLER

Full of Potential

Let him who would enjoy a good future
waste none of his present.

—ROGER BABSON

Great ability develops and reveals itself increasingly with every new assignment.

—BALTASAR GRACIAN

Curious

*A sense of curiosity is nature's original
school of education.*

—SMILEY BLANTON

Curiosity will conquer fear even more than bravery will.

—JAMES STEPHENS

. . . *curiosity can be vivid and wholesome only in proportion as the mind is contented and happy.*

—ANATOLE FRANCE

Humble

Whoever loves becomes humble.

—SIGMUND FREUD

Real excellence and humility are not incompatible one with the other, on the contrary they are twin sisters.

—Jean Baptiste Lacordaire

Loyal

There is no faith which has never yet been broken, except that of a truly faithful dog.

—KONRAD LORENZ

Animals are reliable, many full of love, true in their
affections, predictable in their actions, grateful and loyal.
Difficult standards for people to live up to.

—ALFRED A. MONTAPERT

Histories are more full of examples of the fidelity of dogs than of friends.

—ALEXANDER POPE

Friendly

Always hold your head up, but be careful to keep your nose at a friendly level.

—MAX L. FORMAN

A friend is somebody you want to be around when you feel like being by yourself.

—BARBARA BURROW

The greatest sweetener in life is friendship.

—JOSEPH ADDISON

Companions

*Dogs love company. They place it first
on their short list of needs.*

—J.R. ACKERLEY

The love between dog and man is idyllic; dogs were never expelled from paradise.

—Milan Kundera

Little friends may prove great friends.

—Aesop

Commitment

Energy and persistence conquer all things.

—BENJAMIN FRANKLIN

Dogs are the only creatures fitted to serve us beyond the call of duty.

—C.W. MEISTERFELD

He is able who thinks he is able.

—BUDDHA

*Do not dwell in the past, do not dream of the future,
concentrate the mind on the present moment.*

—BUDDHA

Teamwork

Life is much less a competitive struggle for survival than a triumph of cooperation and creativity.

—FRITJOF CAPRA

A sense of share is not a bad moral compass.

—Colin Powell

Affectionate

*Our sweetest experiences of affection are
meant to point us to that realm which is the
real and endless home of the heart.*

—HENRY WARD BEECHER

It is hard for the face to conceal the thoughts of the heart—
the true character of the soul.—The look without is an
index of what is within.

—WILLIAM SHAKESPEARE

We are shaped and fashioned by what we love.

—JOHANN WOLFGANG VON GOETHE

No act of kindness, no matter how small, is ever wasted.

—AESOP

Man while he loves is never quite depraved.

—CHARLES LAMB

Trusting

The best proof of love is trust.

—DR. JOYCE BROTHERS

It is better to suffer wrong than to do it, and happier to be sometimes cheated than not to trust.

—Samuel Johnson

Faith is not belief without proof, but trust without reservation.

—D. Elton Trueblood

Playful

*The time you enjoy wasting is
not wasted time.*

—BERTRAND RUSSELL

The dog was created especially for children. He is the God of frolic.

—Henry Ward Beecher

Not life, but good life, is to be chiefly valued.

—SOCRATES

Accomplished

*A life spent worthily should be
measured by deeds, not years.*

—RICHARD BRINSLEY SHERIDAN

Success is the sum of small efforts—repeated day in and day out.

—ROBERT COLLIER

The secret of joy in work is contained in one word —
excellence. To know how to do something well is to enjoy it.

—PEARL S. BUCK

It takes little talent to see clearly what lies under one's nose, a good deal of it to know in which direction to point that organ.

—W.H. AUDEN

Enthusiasm

Living with a dog is easy—like living with an idealist.

—H.L. Mencken

Nothing is so contagious as enthusiasm.

—EDWARD GEORGE BULWER-LYTTON

Nature loves a burst of energy.

—Boe Lightman

. . . *to have played and laughed with enthusiasm, and sung with exultation; to know even one life has breathed easier because you have lived — this is to have succeeded.*

—RALPH WALDO EMERSON